Don Paterson was born in Dundee in 1963. He works as a musician, and co-leads the jazz-folk ensemble Lammas. He currently divides his time between London and Scotland.

by the same author

NIL NIL

DON PATERSON

God's Gift to Women

faber and faber

First published in 1997
by Faber and Faber Limited
3 Queen Square London WC1N 3AU

Photoset by Wilmaset Ltd, Wirral
Printed in England by Mackays of Chatham PLC, Chatham, Kent

Don Paterson is hereby identified as author of this
work in accordance with Section 77 of the Copyright,
Designs and Patents Act 1988

A CIP record for this book
is available from the British Library

ISBN 0-571-17762-X

2 4 6 8 10 9 7 5 3 1

for Steve and Louise

You may have noticed that a dead fish floats on its back?
Well, a wooden fish can have this same peculiarity, as you
will see if you make this toy.

E. M. Goodrick, Fun for One

Further precisions are given concerning the worship of
divinities such as Janus, Pecunia, Bacchus, Saturn, Mercury,
Mars and Apollo. Obscene rites in honour of the Great
Mother are described in some detail. Attempts at a
naturalistic revision of paganism are not successful. The
gloom is lightened by an atrocious pun. Varro produced a
theology full of learned errors.

St Augustine, City of God (abridged version):
summary of omitted chapters, Book 2, viii–xxiv

Acknowledgements are due to the editors of the following publications and anthologies, where many of the poems first appeared: *Thumbscrew, Oar, Columbia, TLS, Verse, Poetry Review, The North, Cambridge Poetry, The Sunday Times, The Rialto, Southfields, Klaonica: Poems for Bosnia, Emergency Kit, Soho Square VII: New Scottish Writing, British Council New Writing, Waterstone's Guide to Poetry* and *How Poets Work*. Most of the Dundee–Newtyle poems were broadcast in a film made by Kate Bannatyne for BBC Scotland.

Contents

Prologue

A poem is a little church, remember,
you, its congregation, I, its cantor;

so please, no flash, no necking in the pew,
or snorting just to let your neighbour know

you get the clever stuff, or eyeing the watch,
or rustling the wee poke of butterscotch

you'd brought to charm the sour edge off the sermon.
Be upstanding. Now: let us raise the fucking *tone*.

Today, from this holy place of heightened speech,
we will join the berry-bus in its approach

to that sunless pit of rancour and alarm
where language finds its least prestigious form.

Fear not: this is spiritual transport,
albeit the less elevated sort;

while the coach will limp towards its final stage
beyond the snowy graveyard of the page,

no one will leave the premises. In hell,
the tingle-test is inapplicable,

though the sensitives among you may discern
the secondary symptoms: light sweats, heartburn,

that sad thrill in the soft part of the instep
as you crane your neck to size up the long drop.

In the meantime, we will pass round the Big Plate
and should it come back slightly underweight

you will learn the meaning of the Silent Collection,
for our roof leaks, and the organ lacks conviction.

My little church is neither high nor broad,
so get your heads down. Let us pray. Oh God

(i)

10.45: Dundee Ward Road

Addenda

Scott Paterson, b. – d. Oct. '65

(i)

The Gellyburn is six feet under;
they sunk a pipe between its banks,
tricked it in and turfed it over.
We heard it rush from stank to stank,
Ardler Wood to the Caird Estate.

Scott said when you crossed the river
you saw sparks; if you ran at it
something snagged on the line of water.

(ii)

It was Scott who found the one loose knot
from the thousand dead eyes in the fence,
and inside, the tiny silver lochan
with lilies, green rushes, and four swans.
A true artist, he set his pitch:

uncorking the little show for tuppence
he'd count a minute on his watch
while a boy set his eye to the light.

One week he was early, and turned up
at the Foot Clinic in Kemback Street
to see a little girl parade
before the Indian doctor, stripped
down to just her underthings.

Now he dreams about her every night
working through his stretches: *The Mermaid*;
The Swan; *The Tightrope-Walker*; *Wings*.

They leave the party, arm in arm
to a smore so thick, her voice comes
to him as if from a small room;
their footprints in the creaking snow
the love-pact they affirm and reaffirm.

Open for fags, the blazing kiosk
crowns old Jock in asterisks.
He is a saint, and Scott tells him so.

00:00: Law Tunnel

*(leased to the Scottish Mushroom Company
after its closure in 1927)*

(i)

In the airy lull
between the wars
they cut the rails
and closed the doors

on the stalled freight:
crate on crate
of blood and earth –
the shallow berth

of the innocents,
their long room
stale and tense
with the same dream

(ii)

Strewn among
the ragged queue –
the snoring king
and his retinue,

Fenrir, Pol Pot,
Captain Oates
and the leprechauns –
are the teeth, the bones

[6]

and begging-cup
of the drunken piper.
The rats boiled up
below the sleepers

(iii)

The crippled boy
of Hamelin
pounds away
at the locked mountain

waist-deep in thorn
and all forlorn,
he tries to force
the buried doors

I will go to my mother
and sing of my shame
I will grow up to father
the race of the lame

from 1001 Nights: The Early Years

Dawn, and I woke up grieving for my arm
long dead below the little drunken carcass
still shut in her drunk dream. In mine, I recall,
I was fixing a stamp in a savings-book, half-full
of the same heavenly profile, a vast harem
of sisters, each one day younger than the last ...

Heaven, to bed the same new wife each night!
And I try; but morning always brings her back
changed, although I recognise the room:
my puddled suit, her dog-eared Kerouac,
the snot-stream of a knotted Fetherlite
draped on the wineglass. I killed the alarm,

then took her head off with the kitchen knife
and no more malice than I might a rose
for my daily buttonhole. One hand, like a leaf,
still flutters in half-hearted valediction.
I am presently facing the wall, nose-to-nose
with Keanu Reeves. It is a sad reflection.

The Scale of Intensity

1) Not felt. Smoke still rises vertically. In sensitive individuals, déjà vu, mild amnesia. Sea like a mirror.

2) Detected by persons at rest or favourably placed, i.e. in upper floors, hammocks, cathedrals, etc. Leaves rustle.

3) Light sleepers wake. Glasses chink. Hairpins, paperclips display slight magnetic properties. Irritability. Vibration like passing of light trucks.

4) Small bells ring. Small increase in surface tension and viscosity of certain liquids. Domestic violence. Furniture overturned.

5) Heavy sleepers wake. Pendulum clocks stop. Public demonstrations. Large flags fly. Vibration like passing of heavy trucks.

6) Large bells ring. Bookburning. Aurora visible in daylight hours. Unprovoked assaults on strangers. Glassware broken. Loose tiles fly from roof.

7) Weak chimneys broken off at roofline. Waves on small ponds, water turbid with mud. Unprovoked assaults on neighbours. Large static charges built up on windows, mirrors, television screens.

8) Perceptible increase in weight of stationary objects: books, cups, pens heavy to lift. Fall of stucco and some masonry.

Systematic rape of women and young girls. Sand craters.
Cracks in wet ground.

9) Small trees uprooted. Bathwater drains in reverse vortex.
Wholesale slaughter of religious and ethnic minorities.
Conspicuous cracks in ground. Damage to reservoirs and
underground pipelines.

10) Large trees uprooted. Measurable tide in puddles,
teacups, etc. Torture and rape of small children. Irreparable
damage to foundations. Rails bend. Sand shifts horizontally
on beaches.

11) Standing impossible. Widespread self-mutilation.
Corposant visible on pylons, lampposts, metal railings.
Waves seen on ground surface. Most bridges destroyed.

12) Damage total. Movement of hour hand perceptible.
Large rock masses displaced. Sea white.

The Chartres of Gowrie

for T. H.

Late August, say the records, when the gowk-storm
shook itself out from a wisp of cloud
and sent them flying, their coats over their heads.
When every back was turned, the thunder-egg
thumped down in an empty barley-field.

No witness, then, and so we must imagine
everything, from the tiny crystal-stack,
its tingling light-code, the clear ripple of tines,
the shell snapping awake, the black rock
blooming through its heart like boiling tar,

to the great organ at dawn thundering away
half-a-mile up in the roof, still driving
each stone limb to its own extremity
and still unmanned, though if we find this hard
we may posit the autistic elder brother

of Maurice Duruflé or Messiaen.
Whatever, the reality is this:
at Errol, Grange, Longforgan, and St Madoes
they stand dumb in their doorframes, all agog
at the black ship moored in the sea of corn.

11:00: Baldovan

Base Camp. Horizontal sleet. Two small boys
have raised the steel flag of the 20 terminus:

me and Ross Mudie are going up the Hilltown
for the first time ever on our own.

I'm weighing up my spending power: the shillings,
tanners, black pennies, florins with bald kings,

the cold blazonry of a half-crown, threepenny bits
like thick cogs, making them chank together in my pockets.

I plan to buy comics,
sweeties, and magic tricks.

However, I am obscurely worried, as usual,
over matters of procedure, the protocol of travel,

and keep asking Ross the same questions:
where we should sit, when to pull the bell, even

if we have enough money for the fare,
whispering, *Are ye sure? Are ye sure?*

I cannot know the little good it will do me;
the bus will let us down in another country

with the wrong streets and streets that suddenly forget
their names at crossroads or in building-sites

and where no one will have heard of the sweets we ask for
and the man will shake the coins from our fists onto the counter

and call for his wife to come through, come through and see
                                                    this
and if we ever make it home again, the bus

will draw into the charred wreck of itself
and we will enter the land at the point we left off

only our voices sound funny and all the houses are gone
and the rain tastes like kelly and black waves fold in

very slowly at the foot of Macalpine Road
and our sisters and mothers are fifty years dead.

Les Six

(i)

with Cocteau (far left); Georges Auric was briefly sent
to Coventry following the 'umbrella' incident.

(ii)

with Cocteau (second from the left), in the 'Chinese'
parlour, *chez* Laloy. One assumes that Poulenc sneezed.

(iii)

with Cocteau (centre left): the six friends share a joke
at de Beaumont's. Honegger obscured by his own pipe-
smoke.

(iv)

with Cocteau (centre right), May '31. Absent
is Tailleferre, by this time heavily *enceinte*.

(v)

with Cocteau (under piano), rehearsing for *Lilith*,
Milhaud having failed to return from Hammersmith.

(vi)

with Cocteau (far right): late-night horseplay at *Le Boeuf*.
Durey is represented by his photograph.

A Private Bottling

*So I will go, then. I would rather grieve over your absence
than over you.*

Antonio Porchia

Back in the same room that an hour ago
we had led, lamp by lamp, into the darkness
I sit down and turn the radio on low
as the last girl on the planet still awake
reads a dedication to the ships
and puts on a recording of the ocean.

I carefully arrange a chain of nips
in a big fairy-ring; in each square glass
the tincture of a failed geography,
its dwindled burns and woodlands, whin-fires, heather,
the sklent of its wind and its salty rain,
the love-worn habits of its working-folk,
the waveform of their speech, and by extension
how they sing, make love, or take a joke.

So I have a good nose for this sort of thing.

Then I will suffer kiss after fierce kiss
letting their gold tongues slide along my tongue
as each gives up, in turn, its little song
of the patient years in glass and sherry-oak,
the shy negotiations with the sea,
air and earth, the trick of how the peat-smoke
was shut inside it, like a black thought.

Tonight I toast her with the extinct malts
of Ardlussa, Ladyburn and Dalintober
and an ancient pledge of passionate indifference:
Ochon o do dhóigh mé mo chlairsach ar a shon,
wishing her health, as I might wish her weather.

When the circle is closed and I have drunk myself sober
I will tilt the blinds a few degrees, and watch
the dawn grow in a glass of liver-salts,
wait for the birds, the milk-float's sweet nothings,
then slip back to the bed where she lies curled,
replace the live egg of her burning ass
gently, in the cold nest of my lap,
as dead to her as she is to the world.

                         *

Here we are again; it is precisely
twelve, fifteen, thirty years down the road
and one turn higher up the spiral chamber
that separates the burnt ale and dark grains
of what I know, from what I can remember.
Now each glass holds its micro-episode
in permanent suspension, like a movie-frame
on acetate, until it plays again,
revivified by a suave connoisseurship
that deepens in the silence and the dark
to something like an infinite sensitivity.
This is no romantic fantasy: my father
used to know a man who'd taste the sea,
then leave his nets strung out along the bay
because there were no fish in it that day.
Everything is in everything else. It is a matter
of attunement, as once, through the hiss and backwash,

I steered the dial into the voice of God
slightly to the left of Hilversum,
half-drowned by some big, blurry waltz
the way some stars obscure their dwarf companions
for centuries, till someone thinks to look.

In the same way, I can isolate the feints
of feminine effluvia, carrion, shite,
those rogues and toxins only introduced
to give the composition a little weight
as rough harmonics do the violin-note
or Pluto, Cheiron and the lesser saints
might do to our lives, for all you know.
(By Christ, you would recognise their absence
as anyone would testify, having sunk
a glass of *North British*, run off a patent still
in some sleet-hammered satellite of Edinburgh:
a bleak spirit, no amount of caramel
could sweeten or disguise, its after-effect
somewhere between a blanket-bath and a sad wank.
There is, no doubt, a bar in Lothian
where it is sworn upon and swallowed neat
by furloughed riggers and the Special Police,
men who hate the company of women.)

O whiskies of Long Island and Provence!
This little number catches at the throat
but is all sweetness in the finish: my tongue trips
first through burning brake-fluid, then nicotine,
pastis, *Diorissimo* and wet grass;
another is silk sleeves and lip-service
with a kick like a smacked puss in a train-station;
another, the light charge and the trace of zinc

[17]

tap-water picks up at the moon's eclipse.
You will know the time I mean by this.

Because your singular absence, in your absence,
has bred hard, tonight I take the waters
with the whole clan: our faceless ushers, bridesmaids,
our four Shelties, three now ghosts of ghosts;
our douce sons and our lovely loudmouthed daughters
who will, by this late hour, be fully grown,
perhaps with unborn children of their own.
So finally, let me propose a toast:
not to love, or life, or real feeling,
but to their sentimental residue;
to your sweet memory, but not to you.

The sun will close its circle in the sky
before I close my own, and drain the purely
offertory glass that tastes of nothing
but silence, burnt dust on the valves, and whisky.

To Cut It Short

(a companion piece)

And here is the great train three years later
hirpling into Vladivostok Central.
We may infer, from its caterwauling,
its sugared windows and scorched livery,
the grievous excess of its final night.

In a dub a half mile up the track
nearby her upturned hostess trolley
lies the headless body of Scheherezade
whose stories would not tally; besides
I had heard the last already.

21:00: Baldragon

The first kneels in a circle of brown grass,
locked on the highest sun, drawing its rays
into the mirrored furnace of his body.
For days, hardly a crumb has passed his lips,
the quicker to advance his dark enquiries.
He mouths a name, and notes that he has turned
half his right hand gold with nicotine.

*

Inside the middle sun's projection-beam,
a rosy aisle from here to Templelands,
the middle boy is basking in his fame,
and lets his luck break over him in waves.
The girl has hooked her thumb in his back pocket.
The leaves stir. Her image flickers slightly.

*

The light deserts the War Memorial
where the eldest brother crouches like a beggar,
one hand to his face, the other out to catch
the rain, scattering black coins at his feet.
There is a tiny blaze on Gallowshill.

*

*Three suns are going down over Baldragon
on three brothers, each born three months apart.
Here is wisdom: explain to me, if you can,
the parable concerning the three brothers.*

Homesick Paterson,
Live at the Blue Bannock, Thurso

So there was me and Lafayette McNab
the month before we tore up the West Coast.
They'd warned us, mind: this cunt had tried to roast
every button-box that played the club –

a five-row dude, they said. Wis he fuck:
jist a half-a-dozen early Shand licks
and the same Scott Skinner riff if he got stuck.
His Ma had pit his shed in wi an aix

and he'd the sort o puss ye'd never tire o hittin,
but sharp threads: mohair minikilt, wee brogues
wi leather tassles. 'Mind if I sit in?'
I looks over at McNab. He shrugs.

Six numbers later, he's on his fifteenth chorus
o 'Kailyard Blues', gien it *genius is pain*,
eyes screwed shut, pretendin tae ignore us.
So Eh'm gaun tartan cuin' the head back in

when Lafayette stands up, leans over, flashes
this big neep gully fae his jacket, slashes
the boy's bellows up the middle – chiv posed,
erse on stool before his hi-hat's closed.

Meanwhile, he's still dyin o constipation
but that's soon sorted – cos next big squeeze
his box is futterin like a coo's erse, wi the soon-
effects tae match. The hoose is on its knees.

Some axe, mind: a JS Custom Thunderbass,
the '62, with triple reeds and rhinestones.
White as a sheet, he pits it in his furry case
and marches oot. They huvnae seen him since.

High Fives, 'Take the A-Road', then a break.
So here's me heading for the Vladimir
when I gets this waft o Consulate. 'Hey . . . Hameseek . . . '
Sure enough, jist the wey Eh'd left her,

nursin a half o Irn Bru and tequila,
fannin hersel doon wi the *People's Friend*.
'Lang time.' No sae lang's Eh dinna mind.
'Cat goat yer tongue? Ye were aye a queer-like fella . . .

but wee man, dye ken, you were the best?'
'Sorry doll,' says I. *'Nae requests.'*

The Undead

O Lord, forgive him the ingratitude –
but should he celebrate their second lease of life
tonight, rising bloodless as the moon
above the Travel Lodge – his black harp zipped
inside his one black wing – to hit the roads
again, while she rides out the night, walled up
with the corpse on the settee, the dead phone
and the frozen wristwatch, frightened as the wife
alive again amongst her own grave-goods?

Buggery

At round about four months or so
– the time is getting shorter –
I look down as the face below
goes sliding underwater

and though I know it's over with
and she is miles from me
I stay a while to mine the earth
for what was lost at sea

as if the faces of the drowned
might turn up in the harrow:
hold me when I hold you down
and plough the lonely furrow

God's Gift to Women

'The man seems to be under the impression he is God's gift to womankind,' said Arthur. Cradling the enormous, rancid bunch of stock he had brought her, Mary reflected that the Holy Father could no more be depended upon to make an appropriate donation than any other representative of His sex.

G. K. Chesterton, 'Gabriel Gale and the Pearl Necklace'

Dundee, and the Magdalen Green.
The moon is staring down the sun;
one last white javelin inches out
of Lucklawhill, and quietly floats
to JFK or Reykjavik.
Newport comes on with a click
like the door-light from an opened fridge.
The coal train shivers on the bridge.

The east wind blows into his fist;
the bare banks rise up, thigh and breast;
half-blue, cursing under her breath,
the muddy Venus of the Firth
lunges through the waterburn.
You come: I wish the wind would turn
so your face would stay like this,
your lips drawn up to blow a kiss

even now, at your martyrdom –
the window, loose inside its frame,
rolls like a drum, but at the last
gives out, and you give up the ghost.
Meanwhile, our vernacular
Atlantis slides below the stars:
My Lord's Bank, Carthagena, Flisk
go one by one into the dusk.

So here we lie, babes in the wood
of voluntary orphanhood,
left in the dark to bleat and shiver
in my leaf-pattern duvet-cover,
and where Jakob or Wilhelm ought to
stencil in the fatal motto
your bandage has unscrolled above
our tousled heads. Still, we survive –

although, for years, the doctors led
us back along the trail of bread
as if it ran to our rebirth,
not our stepmother's frozen hearth;
when they'd gone, she'd take us back
with big rocks in our haversacks
and twice as far in as before.
But I keep coming back for more,

and every second Wednesday
rehearse the aetiology
of this, my current all-time low
at twenty-seven quid a throw.
Ten years drawing out at the sting
have ascertained the following:
a model of precocity –
Christ at one year, Cain at three

(a single blow was all it took;
the fucker died inside a week) –
I'd wed my mother long before
she'd think to lock the bathroom door,
as much a sly move to defraud
my father of his fatherhood
as clear the blood-debt with the gift
of my right hand; with my left

I dealt myself the whole estate
and in the same stroke, wiped the slate
of my own inheritance. Anyway,
as the semi-bastard progeny
of a morganatic union
(the Mother ranks below the Son),
I am the first man and the last:
there will be no title or bequest.

Once, to my own disbelief,
I almost took a second wife,
and came so close that others slurred
our names together as one word,
a word she gave, a word I took,
a word she conjured with, and broke.
So I filled the diary up again
with the absences of other men:

John's overtime, Jack's training-course,
returning in the tiny hours
with my head clear as a bullet-hole
and a Durex wrapped in toilet roll,
the operation so risk-free
I'd take my own seed home with me
and bury it deep down in the trash,
beside the bad fruit and the ash.

Thus the cross laid on my shoulder
grew light, as I grew harder, colder,
and in each subsequent affair
became the cross that others bear.
Until last night, when I found pain
enough to fill the stony grain
with that old yearly hurt, as if
I might yet burst back into leaf –

O my dear, my 'delicate cutter'
pale phlebotomist, blood-letter –
the back of one, I came home drunk
to find you standing at the sink,
the steady eye of your own storm
feathering up your white forearm
with the edge of a Bic Ladyshave
and the nonchalance of a Chinese chef –

next month, when the scars have gone,
we'll raid the bank and hit the town,
you in that black silk dress, cut low
enough to show an inch or so
of the opalescent hand-long scar
on your left breast. Your mother swore
that fumbling along the shelf,
you'd pulled the pan down on yourself;

but we could see her tipping out
the kettle in the carry-cot,
one eyebrow arched above your cries
as she watched the string of blisters rise
to the design that in ten years
would mark you her inferior,
when all it did was make the one
more lovely than its own dear twin,

as if some angel'd shot his come
as bright as lit magnesium
across your body as you slept.
And as you lie here, tightly happed
in the track-marked arms of Morpheus,
I only wish that I could wish
you more than luck as you delay
before that white-gloved croupier

who offers you the fanned-out pack:
a face-card. The fey and sleekit jack.
The frame yawns to a living-room.
Slim Whitman warbles through the hum
of a bad earth. The Green Lady cries
over the scene: you, compromised,
steadily drawing out the juice
of the one man you could not seduce,

but his legs are sliding up his shorts,
his mouth drops open in its slot
and at the point you suss his groans
come not from his throat, but your own,
it all goes monochrome, and segues
into the usual territory.
You get up from your knees, nineteen,
half-pissed, bleeding through your jeans.

Titless, doll-eyed, party-frocked,
your mother, ashen with the shock
at this, the regular outrage,
pretends to phone the orphanage,
gets out your blue valise, and packs
it tight with pants and ankle-socks
and a pony-book to pass the time
on the long ride to the Home.

And then the old routine: frogmarched
outside to the freezing porch,
you'd shiver out the hour until
she'd shout you in and make the call;
but in your dreams they always come,
the four huge whitecoats, masked and dumb
with their biros, clipboards and pink slips,
the little gibbet of the drip,

the quilted coat with one long arm,
the napkin soaked in chloroform,
the gag, the needle and the van
that fires you down the endless lane
that ends in mile-high chicken-wire
around the silent compound, where
a tower-guard rolls a searchlight beam
over the crematorium –

Enough. Let's hold you in your dream,
leave the radio-alarm
mid-digit and unreadable,
under the bare bulb in the hall
one cranefly braced against the air,
the rain stalled like a chandelier
above the roof, the moon sandbanked
in Gemini. I have to think.

Now. Let us carefully assay
that lost soteriology
which holds Christ died to free himself,
or who slays the dragon or the wolf
on the stage of his presexual
rescue fantasy, makes the kill
not just for her flushed gratitude
but for his Father in the gods:

somewhere between His lofty blessing
and the virgin bride's undressing
the light streams from the gates of heaven
and all is promised and forgiven.
Time and again I blow the dust
off this wee psychodrama, just
a new face in the victim's role —
convinced if I can save her soul

I'll save my own. It doesn't work.
Whatever difference I make
to anyone by daylight is
dispatched in that last torpid kiss
at the darkening crossroads; from there
they go back to their torturers.
But if I could put the sleep I lose
over you to better use,

I'd work the nights as signalman
to your bad dreams, wait for that drawn-
sword sound and the blue wheelsparks,
then make the switch before the track
flicks left, and curves away to hell ...
This once I can, and so I will.
The death-camp gates are swinging to
to let you leave, not swallow you.

They set you down upon a hill.
Your case is huge. Your hands are small.
The sun opens its golden eye
into the blue room of the sky.
A black mare nods up to your side. You
take her reins, and let her guide you
over the sky-blue, trackless heather
to the hearth, the Home, your real mother.

Actaeon

I can see him steal upstairs one night, intent
on fathoming your private firmament
and something, perhaps, of heaven's lottery:
marking the flare of α *Clitoridos*
'that on dark nights casts a shadow on the bed';
the glittery spokes of the Velocipede;

Feles Avidus; the bristling cluster
that they call *Hystrix*, or the Thousand Sisters;
and finally, as he lay there alone
beneath those rainy Pleiads and the gone
moon of the light-bulb, the starless field
where you'd hang him, as a warning to the world.

01:00: Rosemill

An age ago, in broad daylight, it flared
into the tiny bloom of its own name;
now, at even the highest resolution,
no map would pick up on this bald scar
of shattered masonry and mushy beams,
the point of irresistible attraction.

I am floating on the back of a dead star
between the Vidor dump and the Dighty water,
doing it half-asleep and standing up
with a black girl who will wear nothing but black.
A mile back down the line, the points had slipped
to engineer a seamless change of tack

and we left the path without our knowing it,
reeled in, hooked on our own groins. A field
or so away, someone hits the light
in the bunk-space of a clapped-out Dormobile:
the dog chained to the wheel is going berserk
at the white boy being eaten by the dark

but I am Rosemill signal box, my cock
the train drawn up the old Balbeuchly Incline
by means of ropes and stationary engines
to Auchterhouse, where heavy horses stalk
the high ridge, four unbroken miles
till the ground gives, and we freewheel into Newtyle.

The Lover

after Propertius

Poor mortals, with your horoscopes and blood-tests –
what hope is there for you? Even if the plane
lands you safely, why should you not return
to your home in flames or ruins, your wife absconded,
the children blind and dying in their cots?
Even sitting quiet in a locked room
the perils are infinite and unforeseeable.
Only the lover walks upon the earth
careless of what the fates prepare for him:

so you step out at the lights, almost as if
you half-know that today you are the special one.
The woman in the windshield lifting away
her frozen cry, a white mask on a stick,
reveals herself as grey-eyed Atropos;
the sun leaves like a rocket; the sky goes out;
the road floods and widens; on the distant kerb
the lost souls groan and mew like sad trombones;
the ambulance glides up with its black sail –

when somewhere in the other world, she fills
your name full of her breath again, and at once
you float to your feet: the dark rose on your shirt
folds itself away, and you slip back
into the crowd, who, being merely human,
must remember nothing of this incident.
Just one flea-ridden dog chained to the railings,
who might be Cerberus, or patient Argos,
looks on, knowing the great law you have flouted.

Imperial

Is it normal to get this wet? Baby, I'm frightened –
I covered her mouth with my own;
she lay in my arms till the storm-window brightened
and stood at our heads like a stone

After months of jaw jaw, determined that neither
win ground, or be handed the edge,
we gave ourselves up, one to the other
like prisoners over a bridge

and no trade was ever so fair or so tender;
so where was the flaw in the plan,
the night we lay down on the flag of surrender
and woke on the flag of Japan

Poem

after Ladislav Skala

The insolence of it!
Ten years on her trail
and she writes out of the blue.

I'll torch my city flat,
move to the black hills
and begin the search anew.

On Going to Meet a Zen Master in the Kyushu Mountains and Not Finding Him

for A.G.

Little Corona

i.m. Radka Toneff

C: ... true, but there is, however, often a real event which triggers what Jabès called our endocrine fantasies. For example, there was boy in our village, Goran ... I don't recall his last name, but his family were from way up on the Ukraine border ... who played peckhorn or euphonium with the local marching band, and had the most extraordinary skill: he was able to get a tune out of almost anything, and could make a whistle from piece of macaroni, a zither from a cigarette-packet ... Once, I remember, he had us all spellbound as he blew the guts from a goose-egg and then fashioned a kind of primitive ocarina, and on this absurdly delicate instrument blew a strange little off-key melody, almost more breath than note ... I hear it clearly in the lochrian mode of so many of the folk-songs of the region, but this is too convenient to be more than a trick of memory ... Then this scrawny Orpheus, as soon as he knew we were all drawn into his magic, crushed it in his hand, as if out of pure scorn for us; this trick would always draw an involuntary groan from his audience, and the first time I witnessed it I burst into tears ... the sudden, immaculate, irrevocable disappearance of both the singer and the song seemed such a terrifying thing ... I can still see his terrible grin ...

from *Armonie Pierduta și Regăsita: Emil Cioran*, reprinted in *The Aquarian*, no. 12/13, trans. Tess DiMilo

12:00: Dronley

August 20th, 1998, and when I say *Dronley*, I mean more specifically 351/366 on OS *Pathfinder* map 338. Meet me in the deciduous part of the forest, but take the east approach, via Bridgefoot and Templelands. Remember, if God's huge hand were to descend from the clouds or the clear skies, straying indolently over these rough forestry pines, they would feel to him as the pale down on your arm does to me now; whereas the tiny blood-tick that negotiates it – look – rears and tilts like a landrover. When I was two or three, I used to wake up in tears because my parents had such empty faces ... the two lonely eyes, the solitary mouth ... Many years later, I met a man who explained this to me. Most of us have fallen here. (A few – a merciful few – have climbed.) As every adolescent uniquely observes, it's all infinitely relative, then; but a *point* can still exist, the notional singularity from which we can take our bearings, and know how late or how early, or from how far or how high, we have come. So we will talk, or will have talked, in what we will think is silence, deepening and deepening as, one by one, the machines – hitherto unnoticed by us – shut down: the hay-bailer in the next field; the distant traffic from the city; the earth's own secret engines, and then all the clockwork of the heavens, our words suddenly free in the air, as if they were solid print, then statues, then angels.

The Alexandrian Library
Part II: The Return of the Book

For M.D.
the bigger fibber

Before I set pen to paper, a preparative: I close my eyes and imagine myself in another library, where I am sitting with my eyes closed, imagining myself in this one. Being, like most men, far more impressed by the simulacral than the procession of shabby realia with which we are daily confronted (it being only in the former that we ever truly rejoice in the hand of the creator), upon opening my eyes again I affect a genuine astonishment at the pathologically detailed universe my imagination has brought into being. Of course I have done nothing more than return the world to the world again, which is the same as rendering it to God, or whatever deranged Caesar happens to be holding the reins today ...

François Aussemain

The level blue gaze of the lovely librarian
has wrestled your own to the floor,
half-an-hour of her husky insistence finally
coaxing from you, like a long-buried skelf,
the real reason you can't seem to talk to your father.
Beneath the professional concern, you detect
something akin to desire;
though she must let you work, now, and leaves
with a quick little squeeze of the shoulder,
sexually neutral, but somehow prolonged enough
not to oblige you to write off the much-refined
after-hours stockroom scenario
as wishful thinking entirely.
You keep listening, till the bristling efficiency
of her nylons criss-crossing inside her starched whites
has shushed the whole place back to silence.

The tip of your ballpoint is weeping black ink
over the snowy divan of the notepad,
as if it were dreaming incontinently
of the glories to come, but this is the real thing,
and as such it will get the full treatment:
the thirty-seven classical stations of courtly love,
the hymeneal rites of Byzantine complexity,
the Song and the Book and the Film of the Act,
its magnification, discussion, rehearsal,
its almost-indefinite postponement:
for no one has had this idea before –

how you will cherish their tear-stricken faces
the morning you fly the stained sheets from the window!

While shifting your weight to one buttock, silently
breaking the seal on an odourless fart,
you split open the vacuum of black Costa Rica;
the smell of it, capric, deeply provocative,
swims up and wafts itself under your nose
like a flick-knife. You refresh your favourite mug,
the blue Smarties job with the handle still on.
The ghost of your hangover thunders away
(like a train; this should go without saying)
into the featureless steppes, its heart set
on magnetic north; in a couple of hours
it will dock in a small town just short of the Circle,
known dimly, if anyone knows it at all,
for its lead-mines, a dangerous method of throat-singing
and an ardent liqueur, distilled from white turnips
with the taste and appearance of liquid acetylene
and its consequent, utterly perfect effacement
of perceptual borders; two fingers of this stuff
and everything turns into everything else.
At midnight, you tattoo the Horseman's Word
on the back of your wrist with a pin and a biro,
then slip into blissful insentience.
In the morning, excluding the state of your trousers,
it seems there's no damage to pay;
just a stunned vacuity, furred at the edges,
as if you looked out at the world through a big hole
someone had smashed in your living-room window.
A little confused, you spend an hour failing
to scrub the word *SPONG* from your wrist, then set out
for a leisurely tour of the second-hand book-stalls.

Around midday, you notice the demon of accidie
perched on the steeple, yawning contagiously;
you make plans to deal with him, considering, in turn,
a propitiatory nap, the dubbed Polish game-show,
even, roguishly, the hair of the dog.
On the last stroke of noon, he lets fly with the ice-pick
you will wear in your head for a fortnight.

You've developed the habit, at this hour, of randomly
lifting a book from the shelves;
here, there are nothing but books about Art,
that is to say, books with just pictures;
Monday was Twombly, yesterday Watteau,
this afternoon, Balthus: brought to the light,
the brilliant plan you have unconsciously nursed
for the past fifteen minutes turns out to be merely
the prospect of having a wank before teatime.
You will swither luxuriously over a choice:
to swan up, or not, to the top of the building,
then the one extra flight to the glassy enclosure
you share with the brown-winged, probationary angels,
to settle back under the skylight, with Balthus
spread out on the tiles, while the pine-scented ozone
comes walloping in through the vent.
(An atom-sized blowfly goes zipping erratically
across the white field of your conscience, too small
for conclusive identification.)

In the stillness, you make out the delicate jangle
of tiny chimes, thin rods of crystal and amethyst
threaded on silk; to play them, it strikes you,
would feel just like stroking a feather;
it is a universe, advanced in its state

[45]

of chromatic decay, gently disbanding
in the long pole of sunlight that falls from the ceiling,
fixing your jotter exactly. Right now,
if literature were quantum mechanics
you'd be just a sniff from the theory of everything –
one breezy reckoning on the back of a beermat
and that would be that, fuck Einstein. As it is,
with the silence now thickened enough to be workable
and the words ranged like tools on an infinite shadow-board,
each one on the tip of your tongue (i.e. *ranine*),
it is almost time to begin.

The library is losing all faith in itself
– a good sign, you know – as if seconds before
the wall had sprung back from the floor like a pop-up book
to be fingered by God, his hand bracing your shoulder
to steady you as he yanks at the tab
that sticks out of your head, making your writing arm
jerk up and down in big squiggles.
Now everything hangs in the balance,
as if the whole world could be brought into being
by the fact of its clear elocution, as if
the planet now hovered and hummed on the brink
of the great bimillennial switch of polarities
that wiped out the dinosaurs, kick-started the ice-age,
knocked up the virgin, and in the next hour
will deflect the moon out of its course.

Now the last touch: your new toy, '*Infraworlds –
For the Gentle Enhancement of Personal Space*',
a series of ambient soundtracks designed
to be superimposed over absolute silence,
since virtually nothing is on them.

You have *Scottish Renaissance*, *Café Voltaire*
and *Library*, though, as usual, you plump for
Buenos Aires, Early Evening, 1897,
firk out the cassette from its soft pastel cover
and jiggle it into your Walkman.
At first, there seems to be nothing but tape-hiss
though it seeps imperceptibly into the white rush
of steam from a kettle of maté;
through the half-opened casement, a spatter of horse-traffic,
the shudders and yawns of a distant bandoneon;
from a bar on the opposite side of the street,
over the blink of small glasses, two men
discuss metaphysics, or literature;
from previous listenings you know, in an hour or so,
the talk will come round to the subject of women,
and then to one girl in particular;
and end with the phthisical freshing of metal
(you will whack up the volume for this bit),
a short protestation that ends in a gurgle,
the screak of a chair-leg on ironwood parquet
and your man spanking off down an alley.
Till then, you will work.

The new poem is coming along like a dream:
this is the big one, the one that will finally
consolidate everything. It is the usual,
but different: a series of localized, badly-lit,
paradigmatic atrocities seen from a train
at the hour between dusk and oblivion,
but – O his audacity! – rendered as *pastoral*:
the sensitive, paranoid, derelict romance,
the only response that is humanly adequate
now, at this point at the end of the century;

the song that the rest will all find themselves singing
too late, and the words will be yours. You will sue.
It is perfect in length, while your witless coevals,
all keen, when the big flash goes off, to be caught
in the apposite gesture, have spent the last five years
conscientiously failing to finish the epic
or grinding and polishing four lines of nothing
in the desperate hope that the planet will somehow
fall into its transparent curves.

In the poem you appear as a poet, a real one,
with a book out, and two or three gigs in the diary
though neither the taxman, your shrink nor the Gas Board
is having it. Last week, at the manse
for the cosy wee pep-talk arranged by your mother,
the minister, somewhere between the sweet sherry
and the meat-paste and cucumber sandwiches,
leant across, laid his fat paw on your shoulder
and whispered *For fuck's sake, get real, son.*
The train in the poem is rushing you home
as if it remembered what you had forgotten
to water or feed or lock up or turn off;
perhaps you will find the whole house has been stolen,
in its place, just the transom you failed to snib shut;
and what parcel of bloodsuckers, slugs and winged beetles
will the late second post have chucked up on the doormat –
the summons, the X-ray results, the week's notice
of the warranty sale, the genuine death threats
from the jealous, the recently badly-reviewed,
the nutter you met at the workshop?
Now enter the bit-player you think you remember
from the black-and-white Carry-On films, though in your
poems

invariably cast as the louche psychopomp –
widow's peak, wall-eye, BO, the lot.
A full set of obsolete dental equipment
fills his breast-pocket; trailing a fingertip
over the tight row of flame-burs and stylets
he pauses over a mildew-pocked speculum
with which he will take all the time in the world
to find everything wrong with your ticket.
You are describing his hand falling down on your shoulder
    like something to do with a hawk or a lobster
        when his hand falls down on your shoulder
            in precisely the manner you failed to describe,
                and somehow the big switch is made.

The lens flies back, offering a view
of yourself from above, then the two of you, stiff
in a caption of light, the last in a series
of bright rooms, some empty, some spartanly furnished
with their little vignette, like an unfinished strip-cartoon
of which you are clearly the punchline;
then plunges away through the abstracted night
till the train is no more than the pulsating hyphen
in London – Brighton, a jittery point
of no ascertainable hue or dimension
that resolves as the glint in his good eye,
has a half-hearted stab at a twinkle, then fails.
And there, on the page, is the lovely librarian,
the coffee so vividly drawn you could smell it
were it not for the audible whine of his oxters,
his skidmarks and forty years' Kensitas
that admits of no other alternative.

*

They have let you go home. You sit in the dark,
count slowly up to fifty,
then switch on that absolute moron, the anglepoise:
with a sputter of wet wood, the back of your head
explodes in slow motion; through the axehead of sparks
come the horror-waves no one has ever conveyed
without buggering with the typography:
your writing is almost entirely illegible,
and you will never know, since you cannot remember
whether you'd sat in the train or the library,
if it was the page, or your hand shaking.

ENVOI

Someone appears to be using your mouth
to scream through: you shut it abruptly,
oddly relieved to discover the neighbours
pounding the wall, in concern or annoyance;
unfortunately, your house is semi-detached,

that is the gable-end, this is the first floor,
    and, with a bang and a fizz,
here is a door where no door was before
    and where the door was no door is

Postmodern

Boy gets haud o' this porno movie, heavy Swedish number,
  broon-wrapper joab, like. Waants tae mak a copy o' it
but he's only got the ae video machine. So he thinks: Eh ken.
  Gets oot the camcorder that's been lehn gaitherin stoor
in the cupboard since last Christmas, sets it up on a wee table
  right opposite the telly, lines up the screen in the eyepiece.
Nae bather. Lets it roll. When it's feenished he checks the
  start o' the copy jist tae mak sure it's recorded okay. Nae
  sweat.
Dead chuffed wi' hisel. Taks it doon the pub that night and
  lends it tae his pal, then *his* pal borrys it, exetera exetera.
 A fortnight later a' cunt in the pub's seen it, and some boy he
  disnae ken hands it back to him, funny smile on his puss.

Thinks nothin' o' it tho. Onywiy, three weeks later, the boy
  thinks, Ach, the wife's oot, Eh'll hae another squint
at thon video again. Same as before, oot wi' the big box o'
  Scotties, the wife's cocoa-butter, slaps in the video,
settles back in the settee, breeks doon, cock oot. So he's sittin'
  there gien it big licks, a' these Swedes gien it laldy on the
  telly,
when he notices the reflection o' himsel, wankin awa on the
  screen, clear as day. Then he stops wankin. But his
  reflection disnae.
That's cuz it's no' his fuckin reflection. He's only jist taped
  himsel hacin a wank, huzzee. Dye no' get it? Will Eh hae tae
  explain it tae ye?

[51]

My pulse clicks in my throat, so hard it hurts.
The Sunshine Coach will never break through, stalled
for ever on its sad trawl of the schemes,
each rain-dark tenement surrendering up
its palest child. Laid out for little games,
the big house waits with us: one student nurse
and one fourteen-year-old, his forage cap
ablaze with badges: *First Aid*; *Hygiene*; *Fire Drill*.

Gail is lightly braced against the sink,
her face burning, her skirt bunched round her middle
while I try to effect the painless removal
of the inch-long skelf, buried in her flank.
I will not be disturbed; this is heart surgery,
and might well take me an eternity.

from Advice to Young Husbands

No one slips into the same woman twice:
heaven is the innocence of its beholding.

From stroke to stroke, we exchange one bliss
wholly for another. Imagine the unfolding
river-lotus, how it duplicates
the singular perfection of itself
through the packed bud of its billion petticoats,
and your cock, here, the rapt and silent witness,
as disbelief flowers from his disbelief.

Heaven is the innocence of its beholding:
no man slips into the same woman twice.

14:50: Rosekinghall

(Beeching Memorial Railway,
Forfarshire Division)

The next train on Platform 6 will be the 14:50
Rosekinghall – Gallowshill and Blindwell, calling at:

Fairygreen – Templelands – Stars of Forthneth – Silverwells –
Honeyhole – Bee Cott – Pleasance – Sunnyblink –
Butterglen – Heatheryhaugh – St Bride's Ring – Diltie Moss –
Silvie – Leyshade – Bourtreebush – Little Fithie –
Dusty Drum – Spiral Wood – Wandershiell – Windygates –
Red Roofs – Ark Hill – Egypt – Formal –
Letter – Laverockhall – Windyedge – Catchpenny –
Framedrum – Drumtick – Little Fardle – Packhorse –
Carrot – Clatteringbrigs – Smyrna – Bucklerheads –
Outfield – Jericho – Horn – Roughstones –
Loak – Skitchen – Sturt – Oathlaw –
Wolflaw – Farnought – Drunkendubs – Stronetic –
Ironharrow Well – Goats – Tarbrax – Dameye –
Dummiesholes – Caldhame – Hagmuir – Slug of Auchrannie –
Baldragon – Thorn – Wreaths – Spurn Hill –
Drowndubs – The Bloody Inches – Halfway – Groan,
where the train will divide

Candlebird*

after Abbas Ibn Al-Ahnaf, c. 750

If, tonight, she scorns me for my song,
You may be sure of this: within the year
Another man will say this verse to her
And she will yield to him for its sad sweetness.

' *"Then I am like the candlebird,"* ' he'll continue,
After explaining what a candlebird is,
' *"Whose lifeless eyes see nothing and see all,*
Lighting their small room with my burning tongue;

His shadow rears above hers on the wall
As hour by hour, I pass into the air."
Take my hand. Now tell me: flesh or tallow?
Which I am tonight, I leave to you.'

So take my hand and tell me, flesh or tallow.
Which man I am tonight I leave to you.

*Generic name for several species of seabird, the flesh of which is so saturated
 in oil the whole bird can be threaded with a wick and burnt entire

Siesta

i.m. Abel Martin

Now that, halfway home, the fire-fish swims
between the cypress and that highest blue
into which the blind boy lately flew
in his white stone, and with the ivory poem
of the cicada ringing hollow in the elm,
let us praise the Lord –
the black print of his good hand! – who has declared
this silence in the pandemonium.

To the God of absence and of aftermath,
of the anchor in the sea, the brimming sea . . .
whose truant omnipresence sets us free
from this world, and firmly on the one true path,
with our cup of shadows overflowing, with
our hearts uplifted, heavy and half-starved,
let us honour Him who made the Void, and carved
these few words from the thin air of our faith.

after Antonio Machado

Notes

Some of the poems take their titles from the stations of the old Dundee–Newtyle railway (motto: 'Private Enterprise for the Public Good'), which was eventually dismantled in the 1960s as part of Dr Beeching's programme of rationalisation.

Homesick Paterson   button-box – button accordion; shed – hair parting; aix – axe; puss (rhymes with *fuss*) – face; head – theme; gully – knife; posed – hidden; axe – musical instrument; Vladimir – toilet

The Chartres of Gowrie   In the late eighteenth century a local seer, one Thomas Cairnie of Inchture, continually predicted the founding of a great kirk in the Carse of Gowrie that would rival those of Chartres or Cologne. It did not materialise.

The Alexandrian Library, Part II: The Return of the Book   The Aussemain quotation is from *Journals, 1894–99*, and is preceded by the following passage:

> Only when our breath finally fails to cloud the glass shall we apprehend with absolute perspicacity – if only for a few seconds – the true nature of the paradise into which we were born, with each object as an angel, finally freed from its Adamite taxonomy, its adamantine mirror. We inhabit a world of impregnable reflections ... even if, by the child's expedient of arranging two mirrors so as to face one another, we lead the world and its surfaces to their own subtle destruction, we can never find the viewpoint discreet enough to witness the miracle taking place; at the last, it is always the sight of our own idiotic heads peering over the parapet that obscures the vista. Staring into the eyes of

the beloved, we sometimes feel on the threshold of an infinite understanding and tenderness until it dawns on us that we are focused on nothing other than our own tiny, foolish faces, absurdly bloated as on the back of a spoon. The lover, in the act of lovemaking, thinks he is continually on the verge of breaking free, but is always frustrated – his partner is the mirrored door that both shows the way to eternity, and stands implacable guard upon it. Only the poet can swim in these terrible shallows ... he is like a swan feeding on a crystalline lake, his reflection immaculate, his head cancelled utterly as he dives into himself ... dredging the dark underworld for mysteries small enough to carry back, concealed and intact, in his mouth.

02:50: Newtyle

Of this white page, ask no more sense
than of the skies (though you may believe
the rain His tears, the wind His grief,
the snow His shredded evidence